FAMOUS LIVES

The Story of
SITTING BULL
Great Sioux Chief

By Lisa Eisenberg
Illustrated by David Rickman

Gareth Stevens Publishing
MILWAUKEE

Dedicated to my family

For a free color catalog describing Gareth Stevens' list of high-quality books and
multimedia programs, call 1-800-542-2595 (USA) or 1-800-461-9120 (Canada).
Gareth Stevens Publishing's Fax: (414) 225-0377.
See our catalog, too, on the World Wide Web: http://gsinc.com

Library of Congress Cataloging-in-Publication Data

Eisenberg, Lisa.
    The story of Sitting Bull: great Sioux chief / by Lisa Eisenberg ; illustrated by David Rickman.
       p. cm. — (Famous lives)
    Originally published: New York: Dell, 1991.
    Includes index.
    Summary: This great defender of the Sioux Nation had shown his bravery and determination
from a very young age.
    ISBN 0-8368-1465-7 (lib. bdg.)
    1. Sitting Bull, 1830?-1890. 2. Dakota Indians—Biography. 3. Hunkpapa Indians—Biography.
4. Dakota Indians—Kings and rulers. 5. Dakota Indians—Wars. [1. Sitting Bull, 1830?-1890.
2. Dakota Indians—Biography. 3. Indians of North America—Biography.] I. Rickman, David, ill.
II. Title. III. Series: Famous lives (Milwaukee, Wis.).
E99.D1S6035 1996
978'.004975'0092—dc20   95-36799
[B]

First published in this edition in North America in 1996 by
Gareth Stevens Publishing
1555 North RiverCenter Drive, Suite 201
Milwaukee, Wisconsin 53212 USA

Original © 1991 by Parachute Press, Inc. as a Yearling Biography.
Published by arrangement with Bantam Doubleday Dell Books for Young Readers,
a division of Bantam Doubleday Dell Publishing Group, Inc.
Additional end matter © 1996 by Gareth Stevens, Inc.

Contents

A Baby Named Slow

The water of the Grand River was icy cold. The winter sky was a grim, stony gray. But inside the cone-shaped, buffalo-hide tipi on the south bank of the river, the air was warm. A young Sioux woman had just given birth to a baby boy, and her heart was filled with joy.

The new mother's name was Mixed Day. Beside her, an older woman was hard at work. First, she placed the tiny infant on a clean square of deerskin. Then she gently cut the umbilical cord that attached the baby to its mother. She dusted the baby's navel with a fungus powder to protect it, and tied a narrow strip of deerskin around his little stomach. After that, she cleaned the baby with warm, moist sweet grass, rubbed him down with buffalo fat, and wrapped him in blankets.

Once the baby was laid beside his mother, the older woman went to spread the news of his birth. "You have a new baby," she told a warrior who was anxiously waiting outside the tipi. "It is a son."

1

The new father smiled and shouted with joy. Like other Plains Indians, he believed the old saying: A man's most valuable possessions were not his horses, tipis, or weapons—they were his children. And a baby boy was to be prized above all other gifts from Wakan Tanka, the Great Spirit.

Because the Lakota calendar is different from the Euroamerican people's, no one can be sure of the exact date of Sitting Bull's birth. It was probably in March, 1830 or 1831. The Sioux called that time the Winter When Yellow Eyes Played in the Snow. Sitting Bull's birthplace was in the part of the United States we now call South Dakota.

The new baby's father was a great warrior, named Returns-Again because he was always ready to return to battle. He and his wife, who would later change her name to Her Holy Door, were Hunkpapa Lakota Indians. The Hunkpapas were Tetons, which is the name given to the western division within the Great Sioux nation.

"Hunkpapa" means "Those Who Camp by the Entrance." The Hunkpapas and other Sioux tribes were hunters who lived by following buffalo herds back and forth across the Great Plains. Mighty warriors who were fiercely proud of their free and independent life, they were feared and respected by the other Plains Indians.

After the birth of her son, Mixed Day rested for a few days. Then she attended a feast held in her baby's honor. The baby was cuddled and admired, but never permitted to cry. Whenever he opened his mouth to wail, Mixed Day would gently pinch his nostrils together to stop any noise. Allowing a baby to scream was just too dangerous—the noise could easily attract enemies who might attack the camp.

When the baby was about two months old, Mixed Day started carrying him around on her back in a blanket attached to a wooden frame called a cradleboard. When Mixed Day was busy cooking or sewing, she often leaned the cradleboard up against a tipi post so her young son could watch her work. When the tribe was on the move, she hung the cradleboard over her pony's saddlehorn, and the baby rode there alongside cooking pots, sacks of herbs, and other bundles.

On winter nights the baby was bundled up

inside warm, woolly buffalo robes. Often, his mother put him to bed with his moccasins on. If an enemy attacked during the night, she might have to grab up her children and run away from the tent at a moment's notice.

Returns-Again and Mixed Day did not name their new baby right away; they waited to choose a name that suited his personality. In the first few months of his life, they saw nothing amazing about their son. What they did notice was that the little boy couldn't be hurried. When his mother handed him a juicy piece of food from the fire, he didn't stuff it into his mouth the way other babies did. Instead he studied it for a long time before deciding it was all right to eat.

Finally the baby's parents agreed on a name for him. He would be called Hunkesni—a Sioux word that means "slow."

As Slow got bigger, he was taken out of his cradleboard from time to time to practice walking. His father and the other men of the tribe were often off hunting buffalo or raiding horses from other tribes, so the little boy spent most of his time with his mother and the other women and children. As he toddled around among the cooking pots and tipis, his older sisters cuddled him and teased him. The old people of the tribe cheered his attempts at walking, telling Slow that one day he would be a great and powerful hunter and warrior.

Mixed Day and Returns-Again doted on Slow and their other children. Besides his parents, many relatives also helped take care of the little boy. If he started to cry, somebody was always around to give him what he wanted or rock him until he was happy again. No one ever told Slow "no" or gave him a spanking. If he did something wrong, somebody simply asked him to stop. That was the way all Sioux treated children.

As Slow grew older, he became too big for his cradleboard. When the Hunkpapas went on long trips, he now rode in a basket hung under the tail of Mixed Day's pony. By the time he was five years old, Slow rode behind his mother on her pony's back. A few years later, he was given his own pony.

Slow played many different games with the other children in the camp. He rode, wrestled, swam, and ran races. The boys played right along with the girls of the tribe in some games, like the Packing Game. For this, parents made small-scale tipis, *travois* (which are sledges on two poles dragged along the ground by a horse or dog), and bows and arrows for the children to play with. Slow and the other boys and girls pretended to make and break camp, and to cook and hunt, just like the adults. Even though they were having fun, they were also practicing skills they would need when they grew up.

During the winter Slow and his sisters amused themselves with wooden tops that they spun on ice, or they rode down the snowy hills on sleds made of buffalo ribs. When the weather warmed up again, and the snow melted, they often had mudball fights or made blowguns out of hollowed-out wooden stems.

By the time Slow was about nine or ten, he no longer played with his sisters or the other girls, who were now busy learning skills from their mothers and grandmothers. The girls and women of the tribe were responsible for gathering dried buffalo dung, or chips, that they used for their fires. They also had to carry water, prepare buffalo hides for their many uses, sew, cook, hunt for wild turnips and berries, and air the tipis.

Slow and the other boys, in contrast, began learning to hunt. Slow's father, Returns-Again, took him out into the forest and showed him the best type of wood to use for a bow. Slow learned how to cut the wood to the proper size, to smooth it on a rock, and to shape it over a fire. When the bow was polished, Slow decorated it with paint and colored horsehair. When his weapon was ready, Slow felt very proud. Again and again, he went out into the forest to practice shooting arrows from his bow. He could hardly wait until he was old enough to join a real hunting party!

But Slow and the other boys still played games. One of their favorites was pretending to make a raid on a neighboring camp. Apart from the Sioux, there were many different tribes among the Plains Indians: the Cheyennes, the Crows, the Shoshones, the Snakes, the Arapahos, and many others. Warfare between them was part of their life. Stealing and raiding were accepted as the best way to get new horses. Certain tribes, such as the Crows and the Assiniboins, had almost always been enemies with the Hunkpapas and other Sioux tribes. When Slow and his friends played their raiding games, they pretended they were conquering their parents' oldest foes.

In the summer Slow's family and the other Hunkpapas were almost always on the move, following the great herds of buffalo that roamed the plains. When scouts brought news that a new herd had been spotted, the crier, a respected older man, would ride around the circle of tipis shouting:

Many buffalo, I hear, Many buffalo, I hear,
They are coming now, They are coming now,
Sharpen your arrows, Sharpen your knives!

Everyone became very excited. Slow's mother and the other women would race to take down the tipis, pack up their belongings, and tie all the bundles onto the *travois*. Slow was always amazed at how quickly Mixed Day did her work. But everything the family owned was easy to move: Buffalo-hide tipis and bags made of skin could be rolled up into small, lightweight bundles. Instead of heavy pottery dishes for cooking, the Hunkpapas used buffalo pouches, which weighed very little. In fact, they owned nothing that couldn't be carried by a person, dog, or horse.

While his mother and the other women worked, Slow would jump on his pony and help herd his family's animals. Finally, everyone was assembled in a long line, ready to move. The scouts started out first, to keep watch on the buffalo. A few miles behind them rode the most important members of the tribe—the men who had "medicine," or spiritual power, and who could communicate with the Great Spirit. They carried sacred objects to help make the hunt successful. Behind them came the chiefs dressed in feathered and beaded regalia. Finally came the women, children, and old people, and the animals carrying their belongings.

As Slow trotted along beside his family, he had eyes only for the warriors, who rode on both sides of the long column to protect everyone. Warriors had the most high-spirited and fastest horses, and they looked so exciting in their face paint and eagle plumes. As Slow listened to the men chanting their bold fighting songs, his heart ached with longing.

One day, he vowed, he would become the most fearless warrior of all!

The Buffalo Hunt

Slow's tribe traveled about twenty-five miles on an average day, stopping only for rest and food. When the leaders decided it was time to set up a new camp, they looked for a spot that was near water, woods, and grassland which would also provide shelter from the wind and enemies. Once they picked a place, the leaders smoked the ceremonial pipe. After that, the women set up the tribe's tents in a giant circle, where each family had an assigned position near uncles, aunts, and cousins, depending on their importance in the tribe. After the white, cone-shaped tipis had sprung up against the wide prairie sky, the women built fires by spinning the end of a stick against a small pile of tinder. Soon a small flame would shoot out, and the air would fill with the sharp smell of smoke.

Then it was time to eat. Slow's family might roast some meat over the open fire. Sometimes they ate pemmican patties—meat ground together with dried cherries and grapes. The Hunkpapa women's favorite method of cooking was boiling. Buffalo brains and tongues were mouth-watering when cooked in a pouch of water over an open flame. Slow also loved soup made from buffalo hooves or tails.

When everyone had eaten, as night fell over the new camp, Slow would sit around the campfire, listening to the old people tell ancient Sioux stories. He enjoyed hearing the grandfathers repeat the story about Iya, the chief god of evil, who appeared in a cyclone. But even better, he loved listening to thrilling tales of how brave Sioux warriors vanquished their enemies.

His head filled with images from the stories, Slow would finally leave the circle around the campfire and go to bed. The next morning, when the warriors went off in search of buffalo, he would gaze after them and sigh. How long would he have to wait to go with them?

The great moment finally came when Slow was about ten years old. One clear morning, when the hunters went off after a new herd of buffalo, the young boy was allowed to accompany his father and uncles. This was the moment he'd been waiting for his whole life!

Quickly but quietly, he and the band of

hunters rode to the top of a steep hill. Below them a vast herd of buffalo was spread out on the grassy plain. The buffalo, sensing the presence of men, began to grow restless, but before they could stampede, the leader of the hunters gave the signal. The charge was on!

"Hi! Yi!" Slow shouted. He dug his knees into his pony's side and raced down the hill beside the warriors, right into the thick of the bellowing herd. With swift, trembling fingers, he reached for his bow and arrow and took aim at a nearby bull. His first shot struck home. Quick as a flash, he was ready with another arrow. His second shot also found its mark. The buffalo staggered and then fell to the ground.

Slow felt his heart swell with pride—he had killed his first buffalo! Rising up on his pony's back, he shouted for joy. "Hi! Yi!"

One of Slow's uncles rode over to him, grinning. Then he helped Slow cut up the animal's meat so it could be carried back to the camp.

The Hunkpapas used almost every part of the buffalo. Aside from the animal's meat, which they ate, the Indians had many uses for the hide. After tanning, they made clothes and robes from it. They also removed the hair and

scraped the hides thin to use for tipi covers. Some hides were molded into a type of suitcase called a *parfleche*, used for carrying belongings. The Sioux also used other parts of the buffalo: the hooves for glue, the horns for spoons or dishes. They cleaned and dried the bladder to use as a bag for carrying water or food. They made tendons into thread for sewing or stringing beads, and buffalo fat and blood into face paint.

The Sioux were grateful to the buffalo for all it supplied. Slow and his uncle showed their respect for the great animal Slow had just killed. "Thank you, brother," the boy told the bull's body. "My family needs food." He left a piece of buffalo meat on the field as an offering to Wakan Tanka, the Great Spirit. Then, as the Sioux always did after a kill, he turned the skull of the buffalo to face the rising sun, in the hope that more buffalo would be generated for the next hunt.

When Slow returned to camp after his first big hunt, Returns-Again boasted about his son. The other adults praised Slow, too. Slow's heart swelled with pride—a boy's first buffalo kill was a great moment, a giant step toward becoming a man.

In the next few years, Slow was allowed to take part in more of the grown men's practices: Sometimes he danced with them, and he spent more time listening to the adults' conversation around the fire. He still loved hearing the grandfathers repeat the old Sioux stories. But more and more the elders were telling new stories, about the settlers, or palefaces, that some Indians to the south had reported seeing.

What odd creatures these palefaces must be, Slow thought. The Hunkpapa men had smooth, bronzed, hairless faces. Imagine people with skin as white as the clouds! Imagine men with hair growing out of their faces!

Even though they seemed unbelievable, Slow was interested in the palefaces. According to the southern Indians, the white people had strange ways and were not always friendly. Some of these creatures were even now making their way across the prairie.

But the Hunkpapas weren't really concerned, since only a few whites had been seen crossing the plains, and none of them had traveled far to the north. They remained very distant from the Hunkpapas' lands. Neither Slow nor his tribespeople believed they had any reason to fear for the future.

A Brave Named Sitting Bull

When Slow was fourteen, he made a decision: It was time to make the next big step toward manhood. Slow wasn't very tall for his age, but he was strong and husky. And even though he was still called Slow, he'd become very skillful and quick with his bow—he could even shoot a second arrow into the sky before his first had time to drop to the ground.

Slow had also become a fine horseman. Again and again, he'd practiced racing along on his pony and then suddenly slipping down to one side of the animal, so the pony's body would form a shield between him and an unseen enemy. In his heart, Slow knew he was ready to do battle and make his family proud— all he needed was a chance to prove himself.

One day it came. As Slow was walking through the camp, he overheard a warrior named Good-Voiced Elk talking to some other men about raiding some nearby Crow Indians!

In an instant, Slow made up his mind. Without a word to his mother, he slung the small quiver containing his bow and arrows over his shoulder and jumped onto his pony's back. Then, with his heart pounding in his chest, Slow left the camp and followed the war party.

When the warriors saw Slow riding up, they remained silent but raised their eyebrows, surprised to see such a young man join them. But like all Sioux, they had great respect for bravery. Returns-Again, feeling a surge of pride when his son arrived, didn't even think of trying to make Slow go back home. No one knew better than his father just how stubborn Slow could be—it was nearly impossible to make him change his mind once he had made a decision.

But the real reason Returns-Again didn't try to send Slow back was that he admired the boy for coming. He'd always known his son was strong and determined. Now Slow was proving he was spirited and brave as well.

Returns-Again went over to his son. "You may come with us," he said. "Try to do something brave." Instead of a weapon, he then handed Slow a long, thin, decorated stick. This coup stick would be used for a practice called counting coup.

A warrior counted coup in a battle when he rode up right next to his enemy and struck him with a coup stick. The Sioux believed that this was an even more important way for a warrior to show his courage than killing an enemy: Anybody could kill from a distance with an arrow or a gun, but only a truly brave warrior would be willing to risk death by actually touching his opponent. It didn't matter who killed the foe—the greatest honor went to the warrior who first counted coup on him. Three other warriors were allowed to count coup on the same person, but their honor was not so great.

As warriors grew older, they were judged by how many times they had counted coup in their lives. They wore different numbers of feathers in their hair to show how brave they'd been. None of the Sioux believed in being humble about his achievements—in fact, they encouraged each other to brag. But they never lied about their coups.

A boy's first coup was even more important than his first buffalo kill, and Slow could hardly wait for this chance to prove his bravery. He eagerly took the coup stick from his father before he and the rest of the men rode off in the direction of the Muddy Water, the Sioux name for the Missouri River. As they rode, the Hunkpapa warriors watched and listened, searching for some sign of their enemies.

Before long, their scout gave a sign—a band of Crow riders was approaching! Quickly, Good-Voiced Elk led everyone behind a hill, where the men took out their shields and prepared to fight. Their plan was to hide until the enemy drew near, when they would charge out and attack.

As Slow and the other men waited, they made a colorful sight. They had painted their faces and bodies with bright symbols they hoped would bring them protection in battle. Slow, wearing only beads and a loincloth, stood next to his pony, which was now painted bright red.

Slow, so jumpy and excited his nerves tingled, longed to leap onto the pony's back. After all those years of play fighting, he was going to be in a real battle!

Finally, Slow couldn't wait any longer. All at once, he sprang onto his pony, dug in his heels, and charged the enemy all by himself! The other Sioux warriors were surprised, but they didn't waste any time—they weren't about to let a young boy fight the enemy by himself! Jumping onto their own horses, the other warriors quickly attacked along with Slow. But he had a headstart.

The Crows were taken completely off guard. When they saw the band of Sioux charging right toward them, they shouted in alarm. Wheeling their horses around, they raced away, their horses' hooves pounding on the hard prairie ground.

Within seconds, most of the Crow had escaped. But a lone rider fell behind the rest of the band. In a panic, the Crow leaped off his pony and yanked out his bow and arrow. Slow was the first Hunkpapa to see him.

Suddenly, Slow forgot everything he ever learned about battle. He knew he was supposed to drop to one side of his pony to protect himself, but instead he rode straight ahead! In the very instant the Crow was about to shoot his arrow, Slow hurtled up beside him, reached out, and hit him with his coup stick. Then Slow's brightly painted pony knocked the Crow to the ground.

"On-hey!" Slow cried as he thundered past. "I, Slow, have conquered him!"

The other Sioux warriors charged into the fight after Slow. Before long, they had either killed or chased away all the Crows. Slow fought right along with the grown men. When the battle was over, he felt as if he would burst with pride and joy—he was only fourteen, and he'd already counted coup!

If possible, Returns-Again was even more excited than his son. The boy had not only counted coup, but he had been the first to make contact with the enemy in a battle! By these brave actions, Slow had honored his father and his entire family.

As was their custom, the war party rode proudly back to camp, chanting and whooping about their great victory over the Crows. Slow knew he had earned the right to yell along with the men, and his shouts were the loudest of all. Later, Returns-Again covered his son with black victory paint. Then he hoisted Slow up on a big horse and led him around the camp.

"My son struck the enemy!" he told everyone. "He has earned a new, worthier name."

Returns-Again didn't have to think hard to decide upon a new name for Slow. He already had the perfect choice in mind—a very special name that had been revealed to him and a few other men during a hunting trip some months before.

They had been out on the plains. Just after sunset, Returns-Again and the other hunters were sitting around a fire, getting ready to roast the meat of the buffalo they had just killed. As they sat by the fire, they could hear the distant roaring of the buffalo, coming to them over the plains.

Suddenly, they heard someone talking nearby. Alarmed, the men grabbed their weapons, instantly ready to fight off an enemy. Then the hunters watched in surprise as they glimpsed their visitor—a lone buffalo, lumbering toward their campfire. Then something truly amazing happened: The huge shaggy beast began speaking human words!

Returns-Again knew much about spiritual matters and could sometimes communicate with animals. He realized that he and the other hunters were in the presence of the Great Spirit, who sometimes appeared in the form of a bull. Returns-Again alone was able to understand what the buffalo was saying: "Tatanka Yotanka, Tatanka Psica, Tatanka Winyuha Najin, Tatanka Wanjila"—the Sioux words for "Sitting Bull, Jumping Bull, Bull-Standing-With-Cow, Lone Bull." To the Sioux, these terms stand for the four ages of life: infancy, youth, adulthood, and old age.

Returns-Again knew he and the other men had witnessed a powerful event: The names spoken by the great Buffalo God would have spiritual powers. So Returns-Again decided to give up his own name and call himself by one of these names. Since Sitting Bull was the first name spoken by the Buffalo Spirit, it would be the most important and powerful of all. So at that time, Returns-Again had taken the name for himself.

Now he was ready to honor his son by passing that name on to him.

"From this night on," Slow's father announced, "I will be called Jumping Bull—my son will be called Sitting Bull."

Slow finally had a name worthy of a warrior. Surely he would accomplish great things during his lifetime.

A Boy Becomes a Man

The Sioux were fierce warriors who rarely showed mercy to their enemies—they didn't hesitate to scalp the victims they had defeated in battle. But they were also people who had a strong love and respect for the land and the animals that supplied them with the means for survival.

They were very spiritual, too. The Sioux believed that Wakan Tanka, the Great Spirit or Mystery, controlled the entire universe. Wakan Tanka could send spiritual messages to people in many different ways. Often the Great Spirit communicated through eagles, hawks, swallows, elk, deer, or buffalo, and the Sioux believed these animals all had special powers. Some tribespeople, such as Sitting Bull's father, had a special skill for interpreting the signs the animals gave. The Sioux called this ability good medicine.

Like his father, Sitting Bull could sometimes communicate with animals. One day while out hunting, Sitting Bull lay down to rest.

Soon he fell asleep and dreamed that a grizzly bear was stalking him. He awoke trembling and in a cold sweat. He had good reason for being shaken by his dream. A hungry grizzly bear could be very dangerous—a grizzly's shaggy fur was so thick that it was almost impossible for an arrow to pierce it. For these reasons, grizzly bears were considered fierce enemies. The Hunkpapa warriors counted coup on them the same way they did on their human enemies.

Sitting Bull, shaking himself awake from his dream, was about to get up and go home. But suddenly he heard a "yellowhammer," as the Sioux called a woodpecker, knocking its beak against the side of a tree. Instantly Sitting Bull knew that Wakan Tanka was sending him a message through the yellowhammer—the Great Spirit was telling him, "Lie still! Lie still!"

Knowing how important this command must be, Sitting Bull froze. In a few seconds, a *real* grizzly bear came out of the woods, lumbered over, and stared down at Sitting Bull, just as it had in his dream! The boy closed his eyes and without moving a muscle, lay as still as he possibly could. He could even feel the bear's breath on his face! Just when he thought he was

about to be attacked, he heard a grunt. He opened his eyes in time to see the grizzly turn around and shuffle back into the woods.

Sitting Bull let out a long breath of relief before getting to his feet. Then he sang a song to the yellowhammer:

Pretty bird, you saw me and took pity on me;
You wish me to survive among the people.
Oh Bird People, from this day always
You shall be my relatives!

After he returned to the Hunkpapas' camp, Sitting Bull kept his promise to the birds. He began writing and singing more and more songs, and he developed a beautiful singing voice. Sitting Bull was often asked to perform songs for tribal ceremonies and special occasions. His gift for writing and singing helped make him popular with everyone in the camp, especially the young girls.

But as he reached the age of fifteen, Sitting Bull's mind was on other things. He already knew he was someone special—he was brave, he could sing, and he could communicate with animals and birds. But, like all Sioux, he believed that only those who were most pure in body and spirit might truly reach an under-standing with the Great Mysteries of the Uni-verse. To help reach this purity, the time had come for Sitting Bull to take part in a vision quest. Yearning to be a man, he knew receiving a vision from the Great Powers would help him step into adulthood.

A man named Moon Dreamer was the tribe's spiritual leader, called a shaman, or med-icine man. When Jumping Bull led his son to-ward the entrance to the shaman's tipi, the boy was proud that everyone could see he was al-most a man, but he was nervous about what was about to happen. He'd heard stories of the ex-periences other young men had had on their vision quests, and he worried about whether he would bring honor to his family. A boy who did not achieve a successful vision quest could never achieve greatness within the tribe: He could never truly be a warrior without proving he had "good medicine"—supernatural powers.

The first step in the vision quest was for Sitting Bull to stay in the shaman's tipi with him for almost a month. During that time, the boy listened silently and intently while the old man spoke of the history of the great Sioux nation.

He repeated the many stories the Indians had told one another for generations: One of the stories was of the White Buffalo Calf Woman, who had taught the Sioux one of their most important practices, smoking the peace pipe.

"Long ago," Moon Dreamer said, "a beautiful, mysterious woman appeared before two Sioux hunters. She asked them to take her to their camp. There she taught the people that the calumet, or peace pipe, was sacred—that all people who smoked it together must pledge to live peacefully. The woman gave the peace pipe to the chief and walked away. As soon as she was a short distance from the camp, she lay down and turned into a red and brown buffalo calf. Soon, she lay down again, and turned into a white buffalo. Then she changed yet again. This time, she became a dark buffalo."

Sitting Bull had heard this story many times before, but he enjoyed listening to it and the other stories again. Even so, as he learned from the shaman, he couldn't help thinking about the difficult part of the vision quest that still lay ahead.

Finally, it was time to begin the quest's hardest ordeal. Early one morning, Moon Dreamer led the boy up into the hills. While Sitting Bull watched, the shaman prepared a shelter called a sweat lodge. First, he fashioned a dome-shaped frame from willow poles; then he covered the poles with buffalo robes so that the lodge would be airtight. He built the lodge so that the entrance faced east, toward the rising sun, which symbolized rebirth and regeneration.

Moon Dreamer spread a layer of fragrant herbs inside the lodge and dug a small pit in the center of the floor. Then he took the dirt from the pit and made it into a small mound outside the lodge, a short distance away from the entrance. Behind the mound he made a pile of firewood on which to heat some stones.

At last Moon Dreamer said it was time. He had first heated the stones on the fire and placed them in the pit inside the sweat lodge, then he had poured water on the hot rocks to create a steamy cloud that filled the lodge.

Following Moon Dreamer's instructions, Sitting Bull entered the lodge and sat by the heated stones for what seemed like an eternity. Soon his skin was hot and throbbing, and sweat poured down his back and sides. Finally, when the boy felt as if his body were on fire, the shaman ordered him back outside. There he told Sitting Bull to jump into a freezing creek.

Without questioning the shaman's command, Sitting Bull raced across the ground and leaped into icy water, gasping at the shock. As he climbed up out of the creek, he saw that Moon Dreamer was getting ready to say farewell and leave. Naked and without food or water, Sitting Bull remained alone on the hill.

Time passed slowly as the boy sat by himself, trying to ignore the demands of his body, as the shaman had instructed him. But after two days and nights of having nothing to eat or drink, Sitting Bull began to despair of ever having the spiritual experience he yearned for. As the hours went by, he shivered with cold as hunger and thirst gnawed inside him.

By the morning of the third day, Sitting Bull realized both his body and his mind were experiencing a change: He was no longer hungry and thirsty; instead he felt clear-headed, pure, and free of his body. It was almost as if his soul were floating above him, outside his body. With a sense of growing wonder, Sitting Bull gazed upward into the sky. All at once, the heavens appeared to open up, and a great light filled the air. He heard a voice inside him say, "You, Sitting Bull, are in the presence of the Great Spirit."

When the vision had passed, Sitting Bull was weak and trembling. But he also felt a new sense of power and responsibility—he had succeeded in having a vision. As he made his way down the lonely hillside, he could hardly wait to talk over his experience with Moon Dreamer. He knew the older man would help him interpret what had happened.

Moon Dreamer was impressed and pleased when he heard what the boy had achieved in his vision quest. The shaman had suspected that Sitting Bull was a special young man who was destined to be a great leader with strong medicine. This powerful vision proved he had been right. Now, he told the exhausted but joyful Sitting Bull that he was ready to make the final step into manhood: Next summer, he would take part in the Sun Dance.

The Sun Dance

Sitting Bull had known about the Sun Dance, the Sioux's most important religious ceremony, all his life. It was a ritual that showed the tribe's belief in power through self-sacrifice. The Sioux believed that Wakan Tanka controlled everything, and that people were just a tiny speck in the universe. But, if people were willing to go through pain and suffering, the spirits would respect them and might grant them favors.

The Sun Dance, or Wiwanyang Wacipi, took place at the same time every year, in the summer. Grown men of all ages, and from many different bands of Sioux, gathered to take part in it. This year, the preparations began in a month the Sioux called the Moon of the Ripening Chokecherries. Sitting Bull tried to ready himself by listening carefully as the shamans gave him and the other dancers special instructions about what to expect. We don't know all of the details of Sitting Bull's first Sun Dance, but it probably went something like this:

A large dance circle was set up in the center

33

of the Sioux camp. The tribespeople found a special forked cottonwood tree in the woods. In an elaborate ceremony, they chopped down the tree and turned it into a pole, which they painted red, blue, green, and yellow. Then they set it up in the center of the dance circle, and attached rawhide ropes to it.

On the day of the Sun Dance, the shamans prepared Sitting Bull for the ritual. First they painted his hands and feet red, then they painted the blue symbol for the sky on his shoulders. Finally, they led Sitting Bull to a bed of sage facing the sacred pole. There, using a stone knife, they cut two slits in the skin just below one shoulder blade. A skewer was inserted through the slits so that it was fastened to his back by the strip of skin.

While the skewer was pushed through Sitting Bull's skin, he felt great pain, but he knew he would be disgraced if he screamed or fainted. So instead of crying out, he gritted his teeth and chanted a song. Some of the women cried for him and used sweet grass to wipe away his blood. When several more skewers had been inserted into Sitting Bull's skin, the shamans led him to the sacred pole. There they attached ropes from the pole to each of the skewers in his skin.

Once Sitting Bull and the other dancers had been fastened to the pole, the dancing began. Sitting Bull stared up at the sun and sang and danced. The skewers pulled at his skin, and he felt intense pain, but he never cried out. Proud to show how much pain he could endure, he knew he would please Wakan Tanka by proving he could overcome anything.

Sitting Bull kept on dancing until the skewers ripped right through his skin. Knowing he would bear the scars from these wounds for the rest of his life, he rejoiced. A warrior was always proud to show his Sun Dance scars because they proved how brave he could be in the face of pain.

Sitting Bull had now earned his place among the other men of his tribe.

In the years after Sitting Bull's first Sun Dance, he married and began a family of his own, like other men of the tribe. He also gained fame as a great fighter—again and again, he showed outstanding bravery in buffalo hunts, horse raids, and battles with enemy tribes. When he was still in his early twenties, he was chosen to be a member of the Strong Hearts, a group made up of only the best warriors. Rarely had anyone so young been elected to the group.

The Strong Hearts chose Sitting Bull to be one of their sash-wearers, another great honor. As a sash-wearer, Sitting Bull wore a headdress decorated with crow feathers, two buffalo horns, and fur streamers in addition to a special long sash decorated with feathers that he wore over his shoulders and across his chest. The sash was so long that it dragged on the ground. In battles with other tribes, a sash-wearer was expected to demonstrate his bravery by driving a lance through his sash and thus fastening himself to the earth. Being pinned to the ground showed that a warrior would choose death rather than run away.

In the summer of 1856, when Sitting Bull was 25 or 26, his tribe followed its usual pattern of trailing the buffalo herds across the Great Plains, in the states we now call Montana, North Dakota, and South Dakota. When they had finished hunting, the tribespeople decided to steal some horses from a Crow village. The men formed a raiding party of about one hundred warriors, and Sitting Bull, who always loved a good fight, eagerly joined the group.

The Hunkpapas traveled along the Yellowstone River until their scouts spotted a Crow camp. Then the warriors stopped and waited for nightfall. Silently, Sitting Bull and the other men put on their war bonnets. Under the cover of darkness, the warriors slipped toward the sleeping village. As they approached, they could hear only the snorting and stirring of the restless horses they were going to steal.

At last, the men reached the herd and drove the horses away from the camp and off into the night. They made almost no noise, but even so, the Crows sensed something was wrong. Within minutes, they woke up and ran to check on their horses. Immediately, they knew their old enemy had struck. With loud cries, the Crow warriors ran for their weapons, leaped on the backs of their remaining horses, and chased after the Sioux.

Sitting Bull and the others were slowed down by their new herd of horses. When they saw that the Crow were catching up with them, they hastily sent some of the younger warriors ahead with the horses. The more experienced fighters, like Sitting Bull, turned around and got ready to fight.

The two groups of warriors stared at each other. Suddenly, three Crow charged forward, and one Crow counted coup twice. Then a Sioux reached out and grabbed the long tail of the Crow fighter's war bonnet and ripped it. Thereafter, the year 1856 was known as the Year When the War Bonnet Was Torn.

When another Crow rode up and killed a Sioux, Sitting Bull knew what he had to do. He dug his heels into his horse's side and rode straight at one of the Crow leaders, holding his shield and his new muzzle-loading gun. After generations of fighting with bows and arrows and lances, the Hunkpapas were now beginning to use the white man's weapons, too. Sitting Bull hadn't yet learned how to shoot from his horse's back, so he jumped to the ground. Bending down on one knee, he held up his shield and muzzle-loader, taking aim at the Crow.

But the Crow warrior also had a gun. Before Sitting Bull could shoot, the other man fired at him. The shot caused a loud explosion, and a puff of smoke appeared in the sky as the ball smashed through the leather of Sitting Bull's shield. He felt a piercing pain in his left foot, but he paid it no attention. Calmly and steadily, he took aim and fired at his enemy. The Crow fell to the ground and died.

When the other Crow warriors saw that one of their leaders was dead, they turned around and raced back toward their camp. Sitting Bull and the other Hunkpapas didn't follow them; they had the horses they needed—there was no reason for more fighting.

When they rode back to their own camp, the Hunkpapas first mourned the warrior who'd been killed in the battle but then celebrated their victory over the Crow. The chiefs declared Sitting Bull the hero of the battle because he was the one who'd caused the enemy to flee. Even though he was in intense pain from his wound, Sitting Bull felt proud of his fellow warriors' praise. He knew that, once again, he'd shown bravery in the face of a foe.

Sitting Bull took care of his wounded foot after the battle, but it never healed perfectly—for the rest of his life, he would limp when he walked. He would always bear the mark of his fight with the Crow chief.

Though Sitting Bull's reputation as a warrior continued to grow, within his own camp he was known as a sweet and gentle man who always had a kind word for a child or an old person. And he often showed compassion for enemies when his fellow tribespeople did not.

In the winter of 1857, Sitting Bull was part of a band of warriors who raided some Assiniboins, another tribe of Plains Indians whom the Hunkpapas had always regarded as enemies. During the battle, an entire Assiniboin family was wiped out, except for one boy, who looked as if he were about eleven years old. The Hunkpapas were ready to kill him, too, when Sitting Bull came upon the scene. He noticed that the Assiniboin boy didn't cry even in the face of sure death. Perhaps the boy saw some admiration or kindness in Sitting Bull's face, because he looked up at him and shouted, "Big Brother!"

Sitting Bull made up his mind then and there. "Don't shoot him!" he said to the other Hunkpapas. "He is too brave to die. I take this one for my brother."

Some of the warriors argued with him, but Sitting Bull remained firm. He took the boy back to camp and organized an elaborate feast and a ceremony to adopt the child. The boy was named Stays-Back, and he became fiercely loyal to Sitting Bull. Before long, everyone in the tribe came to like and admire Stays-Back.

Although adopting a new brother brought

Sitting Bull happiness, he also suffered deep sadness that same year, when both his wife and infant son died of typhoid fever. And another tragedy occurred the following year, in 1858.

The Hunkpapas were camped near a buffalo herd in North Dakota. They had had a successful hunt, and their horses were grazing peacefully on the green grass. When someone noticed two Crow warriors in the distance, none of the warriors became alarmed. "Stragglers," somebody suggested. "Don't even bother hunting them down."

Two days later, when the Hunkpapas had decided to break camp and move on to a new location, all at once the sound of war whoops filled the air. Fifty Crow warriors were riding over the hill! The Hunkpapas were taken completely by surprise.

Within a few seconds the Crows killed two Sioux boys. But in an instant, the Hunkpapa warriors were fighting back. They shot arrows at the enemy, and when two Crows were quickly killed, the attackers turned and rode away.

A lone Crow warrior stayed behind to fight, however. Sitting on his horse, he held up his rifle and shouted at the Sioux, insulting them and daring them to come after him. The Hunkpapas looked at the gun and stayed where they were.

Sitting Bull had been fighting in another part of the plains, so he didn't know what was happening. But his father, Jumping Bull, was right there. When he saw the Sioux warriors hesitate, Jumping Bull was ashamed. Even though he was now an old man with gray hair, he grabbed his bow and arrow. "*I* will fight the enemy!" he shouted. All by himself, he charged the Crow warrior.

But Jumping Bull's bow and arrow were no match for the Crow's rifle: Before the older man could get close enough to take aim, the Crow shot him in the shoulder. Jumping Bull felt a stab of pain and dropped his bow and arrow. But even so, he didn't stop. Reaching for his knife, he kept walking toward the enemy.

Once again, the Crow was too quick. He jumped off his horse and stabbed Jumping Bull with his own knife. The blade flashed once, then again and again. Within seconds, the older man lay dead on the ground.

In the meantime, someone had rushed to tell Sitting Bull what was happening. When he heard the news, Sitting Bull's only thought was to rescue his father. Leaning forward on his horse's back, he raced across the prairie. When he saw Jumping Bull's limp body, he was filled with horror and rage. The Crow jumped on his own horse and tried to escape, but Sitting Bull ran him down. He took hold of his lance and threw himself at the enemy warrior. The lance killed him instantly.

Sitting Bull grieved over the death of his father. In the traditional Sioux way, he undid his long braids, blackened his face, put on rags, and cried to show his great respect for the dead. He wrapped Jumping Bull in a buffalo robe and placed his bow and arrow next to the body. Then he killed two horses so his father could ride in the land of the dead.

The period of mourning slowly passed. As it did, Sitting Bull knew he could hold his head high in the village. He had avenged Jumping Bull's death by killing the Crow who had shot him, and he had honorably displayed his grief. Even during a time of such deep sadness, Sitting Bull had proven himself to be strong and brave.

One Chief for All the Sioux

In the early 1860's, Sitting Bull and the other Sioux did not take part in the Civil War that was raging in much of the United States. All they wanted was to be left alone to hunt buffalo and live as they always had on their beloved land.

For Indians in other parts of the country, however, this was no longer possible. White people, in their greed for new land, were spreading farther and farther west. Instead of allowing Indians to live peacefully, these white people forced them onto reservations—land set aside for them to live on. Most often, they were smaller than the amount of land the Indians had had before.

Many Indians didn't want to go to reservations. In Minnesota, some Sioux who'd lost their land were driven to the edge of starvation. They finally went on the warpath and killed several hundred white people. The governor of Minnesota sent some army troops, led by Colonel Henry H. Sibley, to fight against them.

At the same time, in 1863, a drought forced Sitting Bull and his tribespeople to go hunting far from their usual territory. When they crossed to the east side of the Missouri River, they came across a band of Minnesota Sioux who were in the midst of a fight with Colonel Sibley's bluecoats—the Indian name for army troops because of the color of their uniforms.

Sitting Bull and the other Hunkpapas eagerly joined in the battle. Though the fighting was fierce and Colonel Sibley's men held off the Indians with their guns, Sitting Bull counted coup once, and he stole an army mule. In his first battle with the bluecoats, Sitting Bull had distinguished himself.

Tensions between the white people and the Indians increased the following year. In 1864, troops of soldiers led by a Colonel J. M. Chivington marched on a friendly village of Cheyenne Indians near Fort Lion, in Colorado. Most of the Indian men were away hunting, but the soldiers killed the women and children who had remained in camp.

It was a brutal massacre. Even the U.S. Government's own report stated that, "It scarcely has its parallel in the records of Indian brutal-

45

ity. Fleeing women, holding up their hands and praying for mercy, were shot down. . . ." Some of Colonel Chivington's men, angered by past Indian scalpings, went so far as to take scalps from their Cheyenne victims!

Later that year, some Cheyennes traveled north to where the Hunkpapas were camped. When Sitting Bull heard of the army's cruelty, he was horrified. The Cheyennes told Sitting Bull they planned to declare war on the white people. They gave him their war pipe, and he smoked it with them, agreeing to join their fight.

Meanwhile, white people continued to move westward, grabbing up land as they went. Most of them had no respect for the Indians' way of life or for their sacred lands. In fact, many white settlers believed the Indians weren't even real people but primitive savages with no rights at all. These whites felt that their own desires for gold and land were far more important than the Indians' claims. They could see no good reason not to open roads and build permanent forts on land that had belonged to the Indians for generation after generation.

During these troubling years, Sitting Bull continued to gain the respect and admiration of the other Hunkpapas. A fierce and brave warrior, he had become one of the leaders of the tribe. Also, he had demonstrated that he had the power of big medicine, meaning that he could communicate with animals and interpret messages from Wakan Tanka. Sitting Bull often had visions in which the Great Spirit told him what the future would bring. His skill was so great that some tribespeople thought he could make the weather and the buffalo follow his orders! Soon his fame as both a leader and a medicine man spread throughout the tribes of the Great Plains.

As the Sioux were growing more and more worried about the advances of the white people, the chiefs of many tribes felt that the whites' threat to the Indians' way of life made it necessary for them to band together. They agreed to join forces, and to select one man to be chief of all their tribes.

Finally, in 1865, at Sun Dance time, the tribes gathered to take part in the ceremony to select this great chief. Cheyennes and Arapahos, who were not Sioux, came along with the

Sioux tribes of the Hunkpapas, the Oglalas, the Mineconjous, the Sans Arcs, the Yanktonais, the Two Kettles, and the Blackfeet.

Sitting Bull was presented as being worthy of the position of chief over all the tribes. The other chiefs agreed that he was the perfect choice.

A special lodge was built for the occasion. Then four chiefs, named Running Antelope, Loud-Voiced Hawk, Four Winds, and Red Horn, carried a buffalo robe to Sitting Bull's tipi. Sitting Bull sat down on the robe, and the chiefs carried him on it back to the new lodge.

Together Sitting Bull and the four chiefs smoked a ceremonial pipe. First they pointed the pipe down toward the earth so it would continue to hold them together. Then they pointed it toward each of the four winds so that no ill wind would blow on them. Last they pointed it to the sun so it would light their way. As they smoked, they prayed to Wakan Tanka.

After this part of the ceremony, the chiefs gave speeches about Sitting Bull. "Because of your bravery on the battlefield, and your reputation as the bravest warrior in all our bands," Four Winds said, "we have elected you chief of

the entire Sioux nation, head war chief. It is your duty to see that the nation is fed, that we have plenty. When you say 'fight,' we shall fight: when you say 'make peace,' we shall make peace."

The other chiefs spoke, too. After the speeches, the Sioux appointed Crazy Horse, of the Oglala tribe, to be second in command after Sitting Bull. Then the leaders gave Sitting Bull a new gun, bow and arrows, and a new war bonnet, decorated with ermine fur and eagle feathers. Finally, after presenting Sitting Bull with a magnificent white horse, they lifted him up onto the horse, and led him around the great camp made up of all the different tribes.

Sitting Bull felt humbled by the great responsibility given him, but he was also proud to have been chosen as the new chief. As he rode through the camp he was moved to sing a song he had just written:

> *Ye tribes, behold me.*
> *The chiefs of old are gone.*
> *Myself, I shall take courage.*

The Treaty of 1868

The next several years on the Great Plains were bloody and violent. Indians from many different tribes, including the Sioux, battled with white settlers and soldiers. Finally, in 1868, the government sent a priest, Father Pierre Jean De Smet, into Indian territory. His job was to meet with the Indians and work out an arrangement to stop the fighting and bloodshed.

Father De Smet traveled into Indian country in a carriage decorated with a black cross. As his party approached the Hunkpapa's camp on the Powder River, runners raced ahead to tell Sitting Bull that a Black Robe, their name for a priest, was coming to meet with him. Sitting Bull sent back this message:

"Tell the Black Robe we shall meet him and his friends with arms stretched out, ready to embrace him. No man living can remember that I ever treated a peace commission with contempt, or gave them hard words, or did them any harm."

On June 19, Father De Smet reached the

great Sioux camp, which was home to several thousand Indians. Everyone came out to see the visitor, and they sang as they followed his carriage. Later, Father De Smet described the scene:

"Plumes of eagles and other birds adorned their long hair and even their steeds had them in their manes and tails, mingled with silk ribbons of various colors. . . . Each one had his visage daubed according to his own ideas, with black, yellow, or blue, streaked and spotted in every imaginable shade."

Father De Smet and his interpreter were taken to Sitting Bull's tent. The Indians gave them food and allowed them to rest. The next day, it was time to talk. "The council was opened with songs and dances, noisy, joyful and very wild," Father De Smet wrote. After the peace pipe was smoked, Father De Smet explained that the Grandfather, as the Indians always called the United States Government, was ready for peace.

Sitting Bull told the priest, "I am and always have been a fool and a warrior, my people caused me to be so." He explained that he also was ready to be a friend to the whites forever after. He agreed to come to Fort Rice in southern North Dakota to meet with the Grandfather's chiefs. But, he added firmly, he was not about to give away Sioux land or trees. And he wanted the white soldiers to abandon their forts.

When the speeches were over, Sitting Bull decided not to go back to Fort Rice with Father De Smet. Instead he sent a fellow warrior named Gall. Gall had always been one of Sitting Bull's rivals for power within the tribe. Once he had almost been killed by white soldiers, and he bitterly hated them. Because of that, Sitting Bull believed Gall would stand up to the government people.

Sitting Bull turned out to be right. At the meeting at Fort Rice, one of the commissioners suggested the Sioux might find their lives easier if they gave up hunting and took up farming as a way of life.

"We were born naked and have been taught to hunt and live on game," Gall answered angrily. "You tell us we must learn to farm, live in one house, and take on your ways. Suppose the people living beyond the great sea should come and tell you that you must stop farming and kill your cattle, and take your houses and lands, what would you do? Would you not fight them?"

But after this fiery speech, on July 2, 1868, Gall and another Indian representative, Bull Owl, did sign a treaty with the white government. This treaty stated that the land bounded by the North Platte River and the Big Horn Mountains would be Indian Territory, and that no white people could settle there. This was a huge piece of land in parts of the states now known as North and South Dakota, Nebraska, Wyoming, and Montana. The Black Hills, which the Sioux considered sacred, were part of this land.

The treaty also stated that the U.S. Government would abandon the forts it had already built in Indian Territory. In addition, the Sioux would be allowed to hunt in areas outside the Territory where large numbers of buffalo roamed. The treaty promised that the terms of the agreement would be kept "as long as the sun shall shine."

For a short time thereafter, life went on as usual in Sitting Bull's camp. As it was the custom for Sioux men to marry more than one woman, Sitting Bull now had several wives. In addition to his own five children, he had

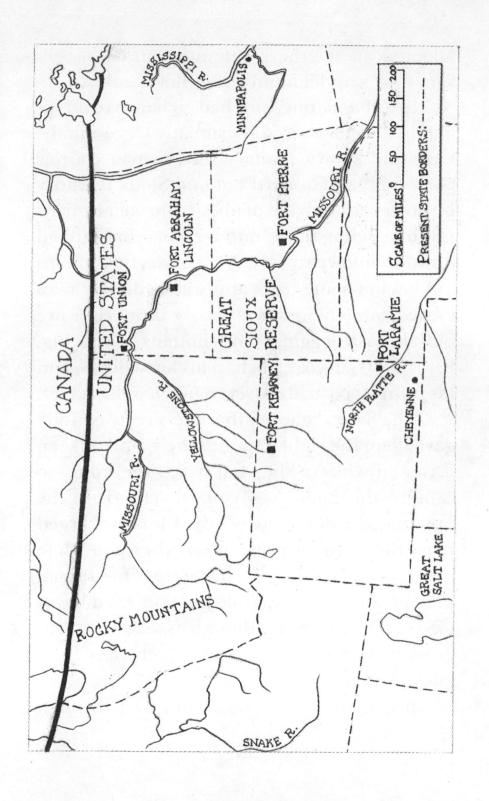

adopted many others, one of them his sister's son, who was deaf and could not speak.

In 1869, Sitting Bull had a chance to adopt another member into his already large family. One cold snowy January day, a mail courier named Frank Grouard entered Sioux territory on horseback. A band of about fourteen Indians saw him riding down into a ravine that dipped down about twenty feet. As he rode, the Indians hid behind some trees and watched. The man looked something like a grizzly bear. He wore buffalo skin leggings and mittens and a big, furry bearskin coat. He had his head down, and his face was partially covered by a handkerchief.

The Sioux believed that the Treaty of 1868 gave them the right to police their land to keep it free of whites. They felt it was their duty to capture this man. As Grouard started up the opposite side of the ravine, the Indians charged from their hiding place, jumped on the white man, and pulled him off his horse. One Indian pointed a gun at him while another tried to rip off his big coat. Even though Grouard fought as hard as he could, he would surely have been killed within a few minutes.

Just then, Sitting Bull appeared through

the trees. The Sioux chief took pity on the man, possibly because Grouard had dark skin and looked like an Indian, or possibly because he was so outnumbered. "Don't shoot him!" Sitting Bull cried to the Sioux with a gun. "Take him prisoner instead."

But the warrior wouldn't listen—he kept on trying to position himself for a good shot. As he took aim, Sitting Bull leaped off his horse and struck him with his bow. The brave fell to the ground, then got up and stomped off through the woods.

When the other Sioux in the band began arguing about what to do next, Sitting Bull took charge. He motioned for Frank Grouard to sit down on the ground next to him. Then he got out his pipe and smoked it with the white man. In sign language Sitting Bull let Grouard know he wanted him to ride along with them.

Sitting Bull, Grouard, and the other Indians rode for three days until they reached the Indians' camp. As everyone rushed out to see the prisoner, Grouard was afraid of what might happen to him. But all the Sioux did was take him to Sitting Bull's tipi, give him some warm buffalo robes, and let him fall asleep.

Sitting Bull called a meeting to decide what to do with the prisoner. Two of the tribe's leaders, Gall and another warrior named No Neck, had strong opinions: "Kill the white man," they said.

But Sitting Bull argued against them. He reminded them of the time he had adopted Stays-Back, the Assiniboin boy who was now using his father's name, Jumping Bull. "When Little Assiniboin was taken from his people, it was Sitting Bull who bore him to his lodge and made him his brother. So with the paleface within the lodge of Sitting Bull this night. He is Standing Bear, the brother of Sitting Bull. My will is spoken."

Because Jumping Bull, Sitting Bull's first adopted brother, was very popular with the other tribe members, they agreed to let Sitting Bull adopt the white man as well.

Frank Grouard stayed with the tribe for three years and learned to speak the Sioux language. Sitting Bull explained to his new brother why he had given him the name Standing Bear. When he had first seen Grouard in his big bearskin coat fighting for his life in the gulch, said Sitting Bull, he'd thought he really *was* a bear!

Come to the Rosebud

By 1870, many of the Plains Indians had moved onto government reservations. But Sitting Bull wanted no part of them for his people. When he heard that Red Cloud, a powerful Oglala chief, was taking part in a council to decide where a Sioux reservation would be, Sitting Bull said, "The white people have put bad medicine over Red Cloud's eyes. . . ."

Despite the Treaty of 1868, it wasn't long before Sitting Bull's people found themselves in another confrontation with the white people. In 1872, the United States Government sent a commission to survey the area around the Yellowstone River. They wanted to use the region for the Northern Pacific Railway, even though it would run right through the middle of Indian Territory! Some Sioux, like Gall, were outraged and fought with the white soldiers who had come along to protect the commission. The Indians knew they were in the right: No one had asked permission to travel through Indian Territory. The government was doing the exact opposite of what it had agreed to in the treaty!

One day in August, Gall and some other men raced into Sitting Bull's camp. "White soldiers are coming up the river!" they told him.

Sitting Bull decided to go to meet the soldiers himself and tell them they had to leave the Indians' land. He chose leaders from the different Sioux tribes in his camp to come with him. The famous Oglala chief Crazy Horse was part of the group.

The party rode to the soldiers' camp, which they reached in the early hours of morning. Before Sitting Bull had time to say a word, the soldiers started shooting. The Indians fought back, and the battle raged on for the rest of the morning. Both Sitting Bull and Crazy Horse were brilliant and brave in their fighting. Although they were unhurt at the end of the battle, they didn't celebrate. They were saddened by the large number of Indians who had been wounded. Together they agreed that they would not do anything to provoke the white soldiers. But if the soldiers attacked *them*, they wouldn't hesitate to fight back.

During the next two years, the building of

the railroad progressed. The Indians called it the Fire Boat That Walked on the Mountains. Gradually the Fire Boat moved closer to Sitting Bull's land.

White people were growing curious about other parts of Indian Territory, too. They were especially interested in what might be buried under the pine trees that covered the Sioux's beloved Black Hills. In 1874, the U.S. Government decided to find out and that summer organized a huge expedition to explore the Black Hills. Many soldiers, miners, geologists, and newspaper reporters gathered at Fort Rice. On July 2, the expedition, which included one hundred wagons and twelve hundred people, set forth, led by a former army general named George Armstrong Custer.

Lieutenant Colonel Custer was pleased to discover that the Black Hills were not only beautiful but perfect for farming. Even more exciting, before the expedition was over, Custer's messengers were coming out of the mountains with the story that there was "gold at the roots of the grass" in the Black Hills. Eager prospectors everywhere started packing their bags.

The Sioux did not share the white people's

excitement. Once again, no one had asked their permission to come into Indian Territory. Even worse, this time the white government had violated their sacred Black Hills. When the Indians found the rutted trail left by Custer's wagons, they called it the Thieves Road and Custer, the Chief of Thieves.

As soon as the expedition's findings became public, white people appeared to forget all about the Treaty of 1868, and miners rushed into the Black Hills. When the U.S. President, Ulysses S. Grant, sent out a second expedition in 1875, it found hundreds of miners already hard at work. No one seemed to remember that the treaty stated that the Black Hills were to be "set apart for the absolute and undisturbed use and occupation of the Indians. . . ."

The government, knowing it would never be able to force all the miners out of the Black Hills, decided it was time to send agents to make a new agreement with the Sioux. These agents were instructed to offer the Indians a choice: Either they would pay the Indians $400,000 a year for the right to mine in the Black Hills, or they would buy the land outright for $6 million.

The government wanted Sitting Bull to co-operate with their agents. But first they had to find someone who could locate the Sioux chief's camp. Frank Grouard, Sitting Bull's adopted brother, seemed like the perfect choice.

About a year before, Sitting Bull had begun to question his adopted brother's loyalty. At that time, the white man left the Hunkpapa camp and began working for the U.S. Army. But Grouard knew where the Sioux were, and he could speak their language. He was happy to take on the job of asking Sitting Bull to come to the meeting at the Red Cloud Agency, where many Sioux were already living.

Grouard's job didn't turn out to be an easy one. Sitting Bull and his followers rejected the idea of giving up the sacred land that had been theirs for untold generations. "We want no white men here," the chief told Grouard. "The Black Hills belong to me. If the whites try to take them, I will fight."

Even though Sitting Bull refused to come, members of the commission decided to go ahead and hold its meeting with any Indians who *did* show up at the Red Cloud Agency. But when they did, the officials were surprised to find themselves surrounded by thousands of angry Indians who felt the same way Sitting Bull did about being driven off their own land. The message was clear: The Sioux would not sell the Black Hills. Nor would they accept the idea of the government's "borrowing" the mining rights for a while, either. The agents had to return to Washington, D.C., to report their failure.

During this time, because of the advances of the white settlers, more people were hunting on the Great Plains. The huge herds of buffalo were now disappearing. More and more Indians, afraid they would starve, were moving onto reservations, where the government would at least give them food, shelter, and clothing. But Sitting Bull still sneered at the idea of reservations and at the Indians who lived there—he called them agency Indians, after the part of the reservation where U.S. Government officials stayed to run things and keep order. Rather than go to an agency, Sitting Bull and his followers remained in the hills.

Soon, the government decided to try a new strategy: It sent out a notice to all Indians, ordering them to move to reservations by January

31, 1876, or be treated as "hostiles." Hostile Indians would be forced onto reservations by military force.

The government order didn't even reach the agencies until late December of 1875, when fierce winter weather was already raging over the plains. Although the notice was sent out to the Indian camps, some never received it. Others received it only after the deadline had already passed. Even those who *did* get the message in time were not able to obey it: In the middle of winter it would have been impossible to take down all the tents, pack up the horses, and transport families with small children through ferocious, snowy blizzards.

In January a messenger brought the government's order to Sitting Bull's camp near the Powder River. Sitting Bull sent back a message of his own. He would consider the order to come in, but he could not do anything until the month his people called the Moon When the Green Grass Is Up, in the spring. Meanwhile, the army was welcome to come into the hills and get him if it could. "You won't need to bring any guides," Sitting Bull concluded. "You can find me easily. I won't run away."

When Sitting Bull's message was received, the government refused to back down. On February 1, 1876, the deadline for the Indians to report to an agency had passed. The government declared that Sitting Bull and his followers were now hostile Indians.

The army decided to send General George Crook, whom the Indians called Three Stars, to deal with the Indians. In March 1876, General Crook and a large fighting force set out from Fort Fetterman in Wyoming, hoping to find Crazy Horse and his band of Oglala Sioux. Before long, the weather grew colder, and supplies ran low. If the soldiers didn't find the Indians soon, they would have to return to the fort.

Frank Grouard acted as a scout for General Crook and his troops. On March 17, Grouard led a small army party to a Cheyenne and Oglala camp on the Powder River. Grouard thought he had found Crazy Horse's camp, but he was wrong. Even so, the soldiers charged the village, burning all the tipis and driving away hundreds of the Indians' horses. "Old people tottered and hobbled to get out of the reach of the bullets singing among the lodges," one witness said later. But by then the men in the village had hurried to protect the women and children. Once the Indian warriors started fighting back, they drove off the bluecoats.

General Crook's troops returned to the fort. But the Cheyennes and Oglalas who'd been attacked had suffered terrible losses. They'd managed to get back some of their stolen horses, but they were without food, shelter, and ammunition. They decided to travel to where Crazy Horse really was camped. The tired band, led by a chief named Two Moons, walked for three days and nights in temperatures below zero. When they finally reached Crazy Horse's camp, he gave them food and shelter. And when he heard that their innocent village had been attacked by the bluecoats' army, he told them, "We are going to fight the white man again."

As soon as spring came, Crazy Horse and his followers headed north. There, at the mouth of the Tongue River, in what is now northern Wyoming, they found Sitting Bull's camp. They told him how the bluecoats had attacked the sleeping village of Cheyennes and Oglalas.

"We are an island of Indians in a lake of whites," Sitting Bull responded. "We must stand together, or they will rub us out separately."

Soon the word went out to all Indians west of the Missouri: "Come to the camp at the big bend of the Rosebud River." By June over 15,000 Indians had gathered at the camp in Montana. There were many Sioux tribes, and Cheyenne and Arapaho tribes, too. Large numbers of agency Indians also left their reservations to join the crowd, bringing with them guns and bullets that the free Indians badly needed. This Indian camp was the biggest in history: Three hundred lodges were arranged in one giant circle.

Thousands of Indians had been traveling north toward the Rosebud River for months, but General Phillip Sheridan, commander of the government troops, knew nothing about the camp. The government had no idea of the strength of the mighty Indian forces that were gathering to fight the U.S. army.

Soldiers Falling From the Sky

Sitting Bull was an important chief in the big camp on the Rosebud, but there was no single leader. Instead many chiefs represented the different tribes within the camp.

At night the chiefs sat in a circle around a council fire. With Sitting Bull sat Gall, Crazy Horse, Two Moons, Spotted Eagle, and others. Although they came from different tribes, they all smoked the war pipe together, united by their hatred of the palefaces.

"We must fight together," Sitting Bull told the circle. "One finger alone is nothing. But five fingers together make a fist."

During the day, Sitting Bull worked hard to remind the others that their cause was just and worthy. With his broad shoulders and limping walk, he strode in and out among the many lodges, chanting at the warriors to be brave. His voice was angry and convincing as he sang, "I have been a war chief. All the same, I'm still living."

In June, which the Indians called the Moon

of Making Fat, the Hunkpapas began getting ready for that year's Sun Dance. The forked tree for the central pole was cut down and decorated. A buffalo skull was placed on an altar. Everyone in the giant camp gathered to watch the ceremony.

Sitting Bull proudly wore the scars of many Sun Dances, but he believed this one would be the most important of all. Earlier in the year, he had vowed to give Wakan Tanka a "red blanket" of blood if the Great Spirit would help the Indians in their fight. Now he planned to offer Wakan Tanka one hundred pieces of skin cut from his own arms.

His adopted brother, Jumping Bull, performed the ceremony. Using a sharp knife, he cut fifty small pieces of skin from each of Sitting Bull's arms. Soon the Sioux chief was covered with blood. He chanted prayers during the ordeal, never once crying out in pain.

When the cutting was finished, Sitting Bull began his long dance under the hot sun. Other warriors danced, too, but Sitting Bull danced longest, staring up at the bright sky as he moved. Finally, after three long days, he went into a trance and fell to the ground.

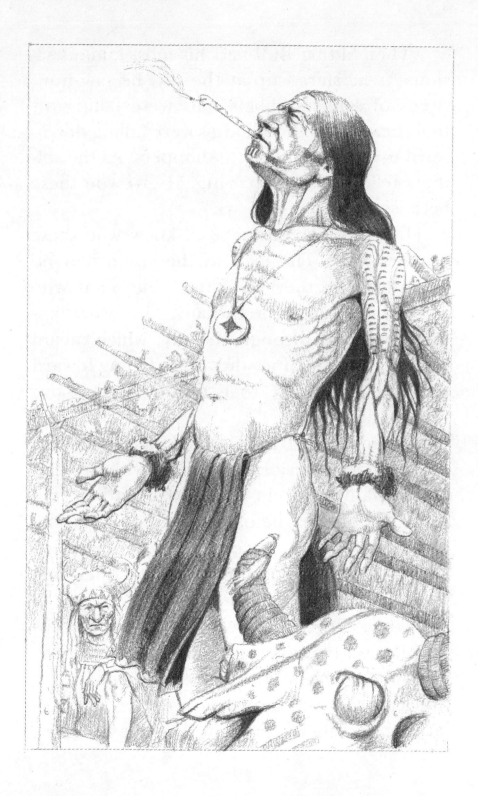

Then Sitting Bull had his most famous vision. As he stared up at the sky, he saw hundreds of soldiers. Their hats were falling off their heads, and their bodies were falling downward toward him like grasshoppers. As the soldiers fell, a voice was crying, "I give you these because they have no ears."

Immediately, Sitting Bull knew who these soldiers were. The men in the vision had no ears, meaning they were the white men who refused to listen to the Indians. They were falling downward through the sky, which meant they were dying. Since they were falling toward the Indians' camp, that meant the Indians would kill them.

When Sitting Bull told the others about this vision, all the warriors were filled with fire and hope. Many of them had heard Sitting Bull make prophecies before, and they knew he could foretell the future. They were sure they would soon be going into a great battle—one which they would win.

While Sitting Bull was preparing for his Sun Dance, the bluecoats had been busy with other things. A month earlier, in May of 1876, the army had begun planning a three-part attack against the Indians, with three different columns of army troops taking part. The troops would be commanded by General "Three Stars" Crook, Colonel John "The One Who Limps" Gibbon, and General Alfred "One Star" Terry. Some of Terry's troops would be led by Lieutenant Colonel George "Long Hair" Custer. Each group of soldiers would move into hostile Indian territory from a different point. By the time of the Sun Dance, the army was already on its way.

On June 17, a few days after Sitting Bull had his vision, a small party of Cheyennes left camp on a hunting expedition. Soon afterward, they raced back. "Bluecoats are camped by the Rosebud!" they cried.

Immediately, a fighting force of a thousand warriors put on war paint and war bonnets. With Sitting Bull leading the Hunkpapas, and Crazy Horse heading the Oglalas, they rode off to do battle. The Indians traveled through the night and reached the army camp in the early morning.

Sitting Bull wore two feathers in his hair and carried a new rifle. As always, he was ready to fight, but he was still exhausted from his long Sun Dance. Crazy Horse took over the leadership of the battle, with Sitting Bull shouting encouragement to his warriors from the rear.

The first fighters the Sioux met with were other Indians—Shoshones, Crows, and Snakes, all longtime Sioux enemies—who were now working for the bluecoats. At a headlong run, the Sioux charged this band of Indians and quickly drove them back. Then with loud whoops and yells, they raced toward the white soldiers.

This group of soldiers was under the command of General Crook. The troops immediately started firing at the Indians, but they just couldn't hold them back. The Sioux would retreat for a while, but again and again they would charge. In the heat of battle, Crazy Horse came up with a new plan. He told his warriors to dart in on their swift ponies and shout taunts at the white soldiers. When the soldiers tried to follow them, the warriors would dash away again.

This strategy confused the bluecoats, who became disorganized when they realized the Indians weren't fighting in the traditional way. They were no longer trying to count coup and show how brave they were—now they were fighting to kill.

By nightfall, General Crook knew he couldn't defeat the relentless Indians. The next day, he ordered his troops to retreat. He wanted to go back to base camp to wait for a message from Colonel Gibbon, General Terry, or Lieutenant Colonel Custer. He now knew that one column of soldiers was no match for the huge force of Indians he'd just fought.

After this victory, some of the Indians in Sitting Bull's band wondered if the chief's vision had now been fulfilled. But Sitting Bull didn't believe it had. In his dream, he'd seen soldiers falling right down into the Indians' camp. But the battle with Crook's soldiers had been twenty miles away.

By this time, the game near the huge Indian encampment had been hunted out, and the ponies had eaten all the grass from the fields. Scouts had been coming in with stories about the many antelope and rich grazing land to the west. Sitting Bull and the other chiefs decided it was time to move. They ordered their followers to pack up their belongings and start out toward the valley of the Greasy Grass.

The Indians had another name for this valley. It was Little Bighorn.

Custer's Last Stand

Sitting Bull's tent was at the far southwest corner of the Hunkpapas' camp in the valley of the Little Bighorn. With him lived his two wives and several other family members. By now, there were about ten thousand Indians living at the camp. One-third of them were warriors. When all the Sioux tribes, including the Sans Arcs, Minneconjous, Oglalas, Brules, and Blackfeet had set up their camps along the Little Bighorn River, the new village was at least three miles long.

Even though most people in the camp had war on their minds, day-to-day life went on much as it always had. The men hunted for game while the women searched for wild turnips and the children swam in the river. At night they danced and sang.

Some evenings the leaders of the tribes held council meetings. All the chiefs were equals within the camp, but one of them was respected above the others. "This was Sitting Bull," explained one Indian who was there. "He

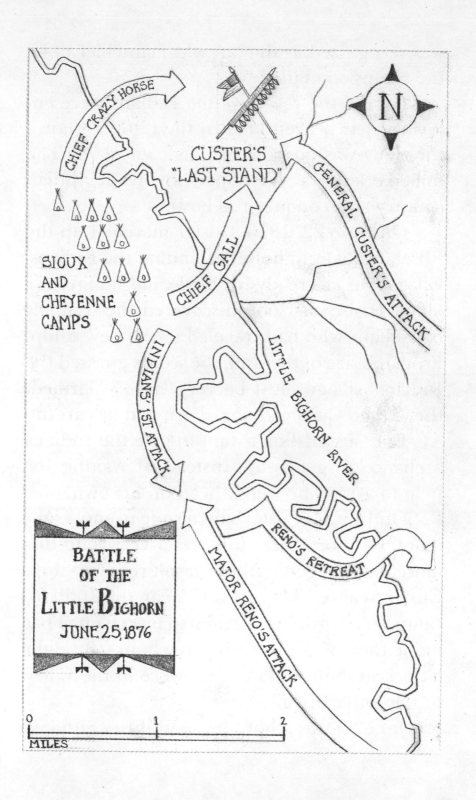

N

CHIEF CRAZY HORSE

CUSTER'S "LAST STAND"

GENERAL CUSTER'S ATTACK

CHIEF GALL

SIOUX AND CHEYENNE CAMPS

INDIANS' 1ST ATTACK

LITTLE BIGHORN RIVER

RENO'S RETREAT

MAJOR RENO'S ATTACK

BATTLE OF THE LITTLE BIGHORN
JUNE 25, 1876

0   1   2
MILES

was recognized as the one old man chief of all the camps combined."

During the few days the Indians were enjoying their peaceful life by the Little Bighorn, the army was busy making its own plans. The military leaders still hoped to invade Indian country and conquer the hostiles.

On June 22, 1876, Custer marched up the Rosebud River in hopes of finding the Indians' village. He was ready for battle and hungry for glory. His scouts soon discovered the trail left by Indians who had traveled to the new camp. From the size of the trail, the scouts guessed the Indians' village must be very large. Alarmed, they urged Custer to slow down and be careful.

But Custer didn't want to give the Indians a chance to get away. Instead of waiting for help to arrive, he went ahead on his own.

On July 24, Custer's men rode twenty-eight miles. On horseback, this was a very long distance, but the general still wasn't ready to stop. Custer realized he was very near the Indians' camp, so he ordered his men to march on. That night, they rested for only three hours. By eight o'clock in the morning, they were in the valley of the Little Bighorn.

June 25 was a hot, dry, and dusty Sunday.

At noon, wearing a coat and pants made of buckskin, Custer organized his troops into three different attack groups: one under the command of Captain Frederick W. Benteen, one under Major Marcus A. Reno, and one led by Custer himself. Captain Benteen's job would be to lead his men through the hills above the valley southeast of the camp and "pitch into anything he came across." Custer's and Reno's troops would proceed together from the hills toward the village before splitting up. Then Major Reno's men would cross the Little Bighorn River and strike the Indian village from the south. Custer would take his men downstream, northward, and attack from there.

Some women digging turnips were the first Indians to see Custer's bluecoats in the distance to the north. They ran to alert the warriors. But by this time, Reno was already attacking the south end of the camp! Although they were completely surprised, the Indians acted with lightning swiftness. When he heard the sounds of the attack, Sitting Bull ran into his tipi for his gun. Then he rushed back outside, jumped up onto his black war horse, and rode out to the front of the pack of mounted warriors. From there he shouted words of advice and support.

Reno's soldiers were stunned by the size and strength of the Sioux force. They jumped off their horses and tried to fight from the ground. But they suffered many losses. "Mount and get back to the bluffs!" Reno commanded them. The bluecoats jumped on their horses, crossed back to the east side of the river and fled to the protection of some cottonwood trees.

The Indian warriors rejoiced at their quick victory. But then Sitting Bull saw a cloud of dust coming from the north and heard the distant sound of a bugle. The bluecoats were attacking the camp from another direction—their assault was just beginning!

Only then was Custer figuring out just how enormous the Indian village was. He hurriedly sent a runner with a message to Captain Benteen: "Come On. Big Village. Be Quick. Bring Packs. . . ."

But Custer's call for help was not answered. On his way down from the bluffs, Benteen ran into Reno's battered and wounded troops. Benteen made a quick decision. Instead of joining Custer, he stayed where he was to protect Reno's men as they retreated from the Indians.

Sitting Bull always liked to be in the thick of

the fighting, but now he knew how important it was for someone to stay in the background and direct the warriors. As Gall and Crazy Horse led the warriors into battle, Sitting Bull stayed in camp, protecting the families, shouting encouraging words, and praying to the Great Spirit.

Custer approached the northern end of the camp, where the Cheyennes had pitched their tents, and they were the first to attack the bluecoats. But the Cheyennes were soon followed by a great throng of warriors from all the different tribes. Thousands of Indians poured out into the valley, shouting war cries, raising their tomahawks, and firing their guns. Custer had only 225 men to fight against them!

When the white soldiers saw the dense mass of shouting men charging right at them, they were horrified. The thundering hooves of the horses stirred up such huge clouds of dust that it was almost impossible to see. Each side shot blindly at the other. Finally, the white soldiers jumped off their horses and fought from the ground. They battled long and hard, but they never really stood a chance of winning.

When the fighting was over, not a single

white soldier was left alive. Long Hair Custer himself was dead. No one knew for sure who'd killed him, though several warriors claimed to have done it.

After the battle, Sitting Bull rode over on his black stallion to survey the terrible scene. When he saw some Indians taking belongings from the dead bodies, he ordered them to stop. His own followers obeyed his commands, but other Indians couldn't resist taking weapons, saddles, watches, and coins. Sitting Bull was saddened by this. He felt that white men's belongings would only make the Indians want to be like white men. He believed this would be a terrible thing for his people.

When the Indians gathered together in their village, they didn't celebrate their victory—instead they mourned their dead. Late that night they held funeral rites for the warriors who'd died in the fighting. They dressed the bodies in fine clothes and lay them on burial platforms. Then they carried the bodies into tipis. Around the tipis, they placed a circle of dead horses so the warriors would be able to ride when they entered the land of the spirits.

Many of the Indians praised Sitting Bull

for having seen the future in his vision of the falling soldiers. But Sitting Bull did not rejoice. What did this one victory matter? He knew that the white people's Grandfather would now be angrier than ever. How much longer could the Indians' cherished way of life go on?

Across the Big Road

Major Reno's and Captain Benteen's soldiers spent the night of the battle huddled in the bluffs where they'd fled that afternoon. They were dirty, bloody, and worn out. But they didn't dare rest—not with thousands of Indians nearby who might attack at any moment. The soldiers worked long hours digging trenches in the hard dirt of the hills. Some of them piled up packs and dead horses to use as barricades.

At daylight, the Indians did attack. They heavily outnumbered the white soldiers. As the morning wore on and the hot sun rose high in the sky, it looked as if the soldiers were beaten.

But then the Indians spotted a new column of bluecoats arriving from the north. Rather than stay and fight, they decided to end the attack. The women and children quickly took down the tipis and packed up their possessions. Then, driving their huge herd of ponies along with them, the Indians marched off toward the Little Bighorn Mountains.

The troops led by Gibbon and Terry had not yet found the Indians. Their scouts, traveling ahead, discovered the terrible battle scene first. When they raced back to tell the commanders, no one believed them. Custer dead? Impossible! But the next day, June 27, when the two commanders finally reached the site of the battle, they had to believe it. Their troops began the grisly job of burying the dead.

By July 5, the news of Custer's defeat and death reached the outside world. "Massacre!" the newspaper headlines screamed. "Horrible!" The stories didn't mention that Custer's troops had made a surprise attack on a peaceful, unsuspecting Indian village. Instead the reporters described the Indians as bloodthirsty savages who wanted to collect white people's scalps.

The United States Government acted fast. Because it wasn't able to capture Sitting Bull or the other chiefs who had fought alongside him, it took action against the Indians it *could* get. In July all Indians who were on reservations in Sioux territory became prisoners of war. In August the government declared that the tribes must surrender huge areas of Indian Territory, including the Black Hills and the Powder River

Country, and move onto reservations. The government had finally found the perfect way of backing out of the Treaty of 1868: They claimed that the Indians had violated the treaty by going to war with the United States! What wasn't mentioned was that the government had never honored the treaty in the first place.

Some of the agency Indians had no choice but to give in and sign a new treaty. But Sitting Bull, as proud and stubborn as ever, still refused to have anything to do with reservations.

The many tribes within the giant village by the Little Bighorn had gone their separate ways, but Sitting Bull still commanded about a thousand warriors. During the summer and fall, he had minor fights with the bluecoats who came into his territory. But the soldiers just wouldn't leave.

Finally Sitting Bull realized that no matter how much he fought for his sacred Black Hills, he would never be allowed to live there in peace. He began to think of leaving the country. "We can go nowhere without seeing the head of an American," he told his council of chiefs. "Our land is small; it is like an island. . . . We have two ways to go, to the land of the great mother [Canada, which was ruled by Queen Victoria] or to the land of the Spaniards [Mexico]."

In October of 1876 the Indians and the whites attempted once more to make peace. A conference was arranged between Colonel Nelson A. Miles, whom the Indians called Bear Coat, and Sitting Bull. They held their meeting on the prairie, seated on buffalo robes.

Miles later wrote that Sitting Bull "was a strong, hardy, sturdy looking man of about five feet eleven inches in height, well-built, with strongly marked features, high cheek bones, prominent nose, straight thin lips, and a strong under jaw, indicating determination and force." He also described Sitting Bull as "cold, but dignified and courteous."

But though he may have been polite, Sitting Bull was very angry. He wanted to know why government troops were still in the area. Miles explained that the army had orders to bring Sitting Bull and his followers to a reservation. He ordered the Sioux to give up their weapons and turn themselves in.

Sitting Bull refused to surrender anything. "No Indians that ever lived loved the white man," he declared indignantly. "The Creator made me an Indian, and not an agency Indian, and I do not intend to become one."

88

Colonel Miles would not budge an inch either. "You will be pursued until you are driven out of the country," he told Sitting Bull. "Or until you can drive the troops out. I will allow you to return to your camp. In fifteen minutes, if you don't accept our terms, we will open fire."

The Indians raced for their horses. The army followed and began firing. A fierce battle raged for two days. The Indians set fire to the grass, hoping to stop the soldiers, but that didn't work. Finally, about two thousand Indians decided to show a truce flag. When they sent a messenger saying they were willing to report to an agency, the battle ended.

Sitting Bull would have nothing to do with the truce or the message. He was still free, but he had now lost most of his fighting force. He and his remaining followers spent a miserable winter on the cold plains. They had little fresh meat since most of the buffalo had disappeared. The Indians were tired, and their spirits were low. To make matters worse, a flood washed away all their lodges in the spring.

Sitting Bull hated the idea of leaving his lands, but he knew it was time to move on. In May of 1877, he and his followers crossed the "Medicine Line," or "Big Road," into Canada.

They set up a new camp in the Pinto Horse Hills, in what would become the Canadian province of Saskatchewan, north of Montana.

In June, Superintendent James Walsh, a Canadian policeman, came to meet Sitting Bull at his new camp. Walsh told Sitting Bull that he and his followers would be expected to obey the Canadian laws against horse stealing. Also, the Indians would be forbidden to go south over the Big Road to make raids in the United States.

Sitting Bull agreed to the Canadian Government's terms, and the Sioux began a life of relative peace in their new home. Although he was homesick for his own lands, Sitting Bull had no wish to return south of the Big Road.

But the governments of Canada and the United States had a different idea. Canada was worried about having so many new Indians within its borders, and the United States wanted Sitting Bull back where they could keep an eye on him. In 1878, the Americans sent Terry to talk to Sitting Bull. Terry told the chief that the Grandfather would forgive the Sioux if they would come live on an American reservation. Sitting Bull's answer was, "For 64 years you have kept and treated my people bad. . . . I shake hands with these people [the Canadians]; the part of the country we came from belonged to us, now we live here."

Terry returned to the United States, and the Sioux stayed in Canada. But life there became harder for Sitting Bull and his people. The Canadian Government would not give them food. The hunting was bad, and the tipis were almost never filled with meat. But if the Indians searched for buffalo south of the border, soldiers shot at them.

Tired of all the problems, more and more of Sitting Bull's people crossed back over the border and went to live on reservations. The aging chief was left with just a small number of the many thousands of Indians who had once followed him. Many of those who stayed with him were either old people or young children.

By the summer of 1881, Sitting Bull knew he and his people would not be able to survive on their own much longer. Something had to change. He asked the Canadian government for a reservation in Canada, but they told him to return to the United States. He made a half-hearted threat to start an Indian war, but the Canadian officers didn't believe him. "I am thrown away!" Sitting Bull said sadly, realizing that he had no choice but to surrender to U.S. authorities.

At about that time, a trader named Louis LeGare offered to help take the Sioux and their belongings back over the border. Reluctantly, Sitting Bull accepted. In July, LeGare brought thirty creaky old carts to the Sioux camp. The Indians loaded up their belongings, and a group of 187 people started its trip south.

On July 19, they rode into Fort Buford in what is now the state of North Dakota. U.S. officers were waiting there to meet them.

Sitting Bull was now only about fifty years old. But he felt old, tired, and sick at heart. Still and quiet, he sat on his horse, his blanket drawn up around his shoulders.

When the Indians lined up to hand over their guns, Sitting Bull took out his rifle from under his blanket. He handed it to his eight-year-old son, Crowfoot. "You take your father's gun," Sitting Bull told his young son. "I surrender it through you. You must learn the ways of the whites and how to live with them. I'm too old to learn much. And remember, your father was the last Sioux to surrender his gun."

The Ghost Dance

When Sitting Bull surrendered, the government promised that he would be given his own place to live and that he would be allowed to rejoin his people on his old, beloved homeland. But, like so many other promises the government made to the Indians, this one was broken. Not long after Sitting Bull crossed the border, he was arrested as the killer of Custer. He and one hundred fifty of his followers were held prisoner at Fort Randall, in what is now South Dakota.

In spite of this unfair treatment, Sitting Bull was not unhappy at the fort. For one thing, his experiences had given him such a low opinion of white people that he had expected to be killed as soon as he stepped back into the United States. Instead, the army officers treated him with respect, letting him continue to lead his small band of followers within the fort.

Things changed for the worse in 1883, when Sitting Bull's group was finally sent to the Standing Rock Agency, in the southern part of North Dakota. Major James "White Hair" McLaughlin, who was in charge of this reservation, decided to take away all of Sitting Bull's power. He described Sitting Bull as "an Indian of very mediocre ability, rather dull." Instead of recognizing him as a chief, McLaughlin put him to work as a farmer. To a great chief and warrior, this was very humiliating.

But Sitting Bull's spirit remained unbroken. He stubbornly went on leading his people, fighting hard to preserve their rights and way of life. Once, when a committee of U.S. senators tried to claim that Sitting Bull wasn't really a chief, he responded angrily, "I am here by the will of the Great Spirit, and by his will I am a chief. . . ."

White Hair McLaughlin kept right on trying to reduce Sitting Bull's power. But even while the chief was struggling at Standing Rock, he was becoming famous in the rest of the country.

The government decided that an Indian should attend the celebration being held in honor of the opening of the Northern Pacific Railway. This was their way of showing that the Indians and the whites were now friends. They selected Sitting Bull because he was so well-known. In his speech there, which he delivered in the Sioux language, Sitting Bull never once mentioned friendship. "I hate all white people," he said. "You are thieves and liars. You have taken away our land and made us outcasts." The white audience didn't understand a word of this, and the interpreter quickly made up a whole new speech in English. The crowd jumped up and gave Sitting Bull a standing ovation!

In the years following his return to the United States, Sitting Bull's life changed a great deal indeed. In 1883, he went on a tour of fifteen cities. In each place he was exhibited as the "slayer of Custer." Two years later he joined Buffalo Bill Cody's Wild West Show. During a typical performance, the Indians would pretend to attack a village while Buffalo Bill and some cowboys galloped in and saved the day. The chief was paid fifty dollars a week for his part in the show. He received top billing over other stars, such as the famous sharpshooter Annie Oakley.

Sitting Bull received mixed reactions from his audiences. Some booed him as Custer's killer, while others lined up to buy his signed picture. Through everything the Sioux chief

kept his usual quiet dignity. According to Annie Oakley, he did not keep his money but gave it away to a group of children who always appeared after the show.

At the end of Sitting Bull's tour with the Wild West Show, Buffalo Bill gave him two presents—a white sombrero and his own favorite gray circus horse. The horse had been trained to sit back on its hind legs and lift one front hoof whenever it heard a gun firing.

In 1887 Buffalo Bill invited Sitting Bull to tour Europe with the Wild West Show. This time the chief refused. "It is bad for our cause for me to parade around, awakening the hatred of white men everywhere," said Sitting Bull. "I am needed here. There is more talk of taking our lands."

Sitting Bull was right. In 1888 a government commission came from Washington, D.C. They wanted to divide the Sioux reservation into six smaller reservations that would take up a much smaller area. This would open up more land for white settlers. The government promised to pay the Indians for any territory they gave up. For a year, the Indians resisted the plan. But in 1889, persuaded by threats and trickery, most of the agency Indians agreed to move to the smaller reservations. Though he lied about it later, McLaughlin didn't even tell Sitting Bull about the meeting where the final agreement was made!

When he learned how the great Sioux reservation had been broken up into six small islands of land, Sitting Bull was enraged. "There are no Indians left but me!" he shouted.

For the next year, Indians on reservations suffered. Drought, crop failures, and sickness swept through the Sioux agencies, and many families starved. To make matters worse, the government never came up with the money it had promised for the Indians' land.

It was at about this time that a new religion called the Ghost Dance swept through the tribes of the plains. On January 1, 1889, Wovoka, an Indian who belonged to the Paiute tribe, had a vision in which he was taken to the spirit world and given sacred teachings. He returned with a message of hope and peace for all Indians, telling them that the earth would be renewed, that the whites would disappear, and that the Indian dead would return to life.

Even though the Paiutes lived in the southwestern part of the United States, their new religion spread quickly. Soon Indians everywhere were doing the Ghost Dance. Wearing ceremonial clothing, they danced in a circle for five days at a time, wailing until the dancers collapsed into a trance and then "came back" from the dead. Through the dance, they hoped Wovoka's vision would come true, and that they would be able to return to their old ways.

In October, which the Indians called the Moon of the Falling Leaves, of 1890, an Oglala Sioux named Kicking Bear came to Standing Rock to tell the Hunkpapas about the new beliefs. Sitting Bull didn't believe dead people could return to the earth, but he didn't mind if his people wanted to take part in the Ghost Dance. He was worried about only one thing: He'd heard that the army didn't like the Indians doing the dance, and he didn't want soldiers hurting his people.

Kicking Bear explained that if the dancers wore special Ghost Shirts, the bluecoats' bullets couldn't harm them. After that, Sitting Bull agreed, and Kicking Bear taught the dance to the Standing Rock Indians.

A week later Major McLaughlin ordered the Indian police to remove Kicking Bear from the reservation. Even after Kicking Bear was gone, however, the Indians kept on doing the Ghost Dance. Government agents on the reservations became more and more concerned. Although they thought that the Ghost Dance was just crazy foolishness, they were afraid that Indians who believed in it might cause unrest. Before long, the government agents made a list of all the troublemakers involved with the Ghost Dance. Sitting Bull's name appeared on the list, and a warrant was issued for his arrest.

Nelson "Bear Coat" Miles, who was now a general, was worried about the disturbance he knew Sitting Bull's arrest would cause among his followers. General Miles came up with an idea he hoped would make the arrest go smoothly: Since Buffalo Bill was the only white man Sitting Bull trusted, he would be the perfect person to take him into custody.

But Major McLaughlin didn't agree. He thought that Buffalo Bill was trying to interfere with his authority, and he resented it. When the showman arrived at Standing Rock with papers saying he should "secure the person of Sitting Bull and deliver him to the nearest commanding officer," McLaughlin tried to stall him while he secretly sent a wire to Washington. But the plan didn't work, and Buffalo Bill set out for Sitting Bull's cabin anyway.

Then McLaughlin came up with another trick. He sent some riders to tell Buffalo Bill that Sitting Bull had just crossed his path going the other way. By the time Buffalo Bill returned to the agency and discovered he had been hoaxed, McLaughlin was able to show him a telegram saying that Washington had overridden General Miles's order. Buffalo Bill left in disgust.

In December a second order for Sitting Bull's arrest was issued. At dawn on December 15, 1890, forty-three policemen came to Sitting Bull's cabin at the Grand River settlement. All of them were Indians. A lieutenant named Bull Head went into the cabin, where he found the chief sleeping on the floor. "You are my prisoner," he told Sitting Bull. "You must go to the agency."

Sitting Bull was confused at being awakened, but he sat up and started to cooperate. "All right," he said. "Let me put on my clothes, and I'll go with you."

Meanwhile, his son Crowfoot ran to tell Sitting Bull's people that their beloved leader was being dragged off to jail. Fearing trouble, the officers tried to get the chief to hurry up. Finally, as they hauled him toward the door still half-dressed, Sitting Bull stumbled. "Let me go," he said. "I'll go without any help."

But the policemen didn't listen. Pushing and shoving, they dragged Sitting Bull out of the cabin. By this time, a crowd of Indians had gathered. They were horrified—their great leader was being treated like a common criminal! The officers poked and punched the chief with their guns. Then they surrounded him and forced their way through the angry crowd.

One of Sitting Bull's wives chanted, "Sitting Bull, you have always been a brave man; what is going to happen now?" Other followers screamed, cried, and shouted, "Kill the policemen!"

All at once, Sitting Bull had a change of heart. His people were watching him. He had always lived as a fighter and a warrior, and he would not stop now. "I'm not going!" he shouted, struggling with his guards.

Lieutenant Bull Head tried to calm him down. "You have no ears," he said, meaning Sitting Bull shouldn't listen to the crowd. He and a sergeant named Red Tomahawk dragged the chief toward a horse.

Just then a Sioux Indian named Catch-the-

Bear pulled out a rifle from under his blanket and shot Bull Head in the leg. As Bull Head fell down on his back, he fired his gun, and the bullet hit Sitting Bull in the back. At the same instant, Red Tomahawk shot Sitting Bull in the head. The chief fell to the frozen ground, blood pouring down his chest. He died instantly.

In the background, Buffalo Bill's old show horse responded to the shots by going into his performance, standing upright and picking up one hoof. Seeing the horse, some of the Indians said it was doing the Ghost Dance. Some even believed the proud, strong spirit of Sitting Bull had entered the horse.

Ferocious fighting continued between Sitting Bull's followers and the Indian policemen until the cavalry, or army horsemen, arrived several hours later. Eight Hunkpapas, including Sitting Bull's son Crowfoot, and six police officers were killed.

But this time, Sitting Bull, the great warrior, couldn't take part in the battle. His struggles to help his people were finished. He died as he had lived, fighting for his pride. And with him died the independent, free life of the once-mighty Sioux nation.

Epilogue

Without Sitting Bull, the Hunkpapas left the Grand River camp and joined the Minneconjou camp. The cavalry forced them to a camp on a creek called Wounded Knee in South Dakota.

On December 29, 1890, Colonel George Forsyth ordered his troops to surround the Sioux. He aimed machine guns at the tipis, and then ordered the Indian men and boys to come out and sit in a semicircle. While some of the soldiers held their guns on the Indians, others searched the tents. They pushed and shoved the frightened and crying women and children.

The medicine man Yellow Bird got up and began doing the Ghost Dance. He reminded the Sioux that the Ghost Shirts they were wearing made them safe from bullets. The soldiers began searching the Indians for weapons.

Suddenly, a shot rang out. All at once, violence was everywhere. The machine guns fired a rapid stream of bullets, killing almost all of the three hundred Indians.

In the years since the massacre at Wounded Knee, life has not been easy for the Sioux or other American Indians. The Indian people experience poverty, unemployment, and alcoholism. Much of their farm-land is infertile. If Sitting Bull were alive, he would grieve for his once strong, independent Sioux nation.

Today, Sioux leaders work hard to improve the lives of their people. They remember the old, sacred ways and keep them alive. Like Sitting Bull, they stubbornly refuse to give up the struggle to maintain the honor, pride, and traditions of the Sioux.

Highlights in the Life of
SITTING BULL

(The dates of events in Sitting Bull's early life are approximate.)

1830-   Slow is born in what is now the state of
1831   South Dakota.

1844   Slow counts coup in battle and earns the name
        Sitting Bull.

1845   Sitting Bull's first Sun Dance.

1857   Sitting Bull adopts an Assiniboin brother.
        His wife and son die of typhoid.

1863   Sitting Bull counts coup on the U.S. Army.

1864   The Plains Indians declare war on the U.S. Army.

1865   The Sioux choose Sitting Bull as their chief.

1868   The Sioux sign a treaty that grants them the
        Black Hills and the Powder River Country.

1876   On June 25, Lieutenant Colonel Custer is killed
        at Little Bighorn.

1877   In May, Sitting Bull and his followers flee to Canada.

1881   Sitting Bull and his followers return to the
        United States. On July 19, they surrender to the
        U.S. Government at Fort Buford, North Dakota.

1883   Sitting Bull and his followers are forced to move
        to the Standing Rock Reservation in North Dakota.

1885   Sitting Bull tours the United States with Buffalo
        Bill Cody's Wild West Show.

1889   The Ghost Dance religion spreads among Indians.

1890   On December 15, Sitting Bull is killed during
        an attempt to arrest him. Two weeks later, the
        Massacre at Wounded Knee – the last major
        battle of the Indian Wars – occurs.

For Further Study

More Books to Read

A Boy Called Slow. Joseph Bruchac (Philomel Books)

The Great Indian Chiefs: Cochise, Geronimo, Crazy Horse, Sitting Bull. Jean-Robert Masson (Barron's)

Sitting Bull. Kathie B. Smith (Simon & Schuster)

Sitting Bull. Herman J. Viola (Raintree)

Sitting Bull and the Battle of the Little Big Horn. Sheila Black (Silver Burdett Press)

Sitting Bull: Sioux Leader. Steven Bodow (Raintree Steck-Vaughn)

Sitting Bull, Sioux Warrior. William R. Sanford (Enslow Publishers)

Sitting Bull, Warrior of the Sioux. Jane Fleischer (Troll Associates)

The Story of Little Bighorn. R. Conrad Stein (Childrens Press)

Videos

Custer: The American Surge Westward. (CRM Films)

Sioux Legends. (AIMS Media)

Index